EVADING ESTRANGEMENT

In Five Parts

Anita Coffey Ouellette

Copyright© 2024 by Anita Coffey Ouellette

All rights reserved.

Published in the United States by Riverhaven Books,

www.RiverhavenBooks.com

ISBN: 978-1-951854-38-6

Printed in the United States of America

Edited and designed by

Stephanie Lynn Blackman

Whitman, MA

With grateful thanks to my first poetry teacher and longtime mentor, the late Ottone Riccio, to whom I brought my first poem, and to my husband Bob who has been the first reader of every poem since.

Contents

I. Beneath Our Common Sky 1
    Queen Anne's Lace 3
    We Are All in the Waiting Room 4
    I wish I could tell you 5
    All weekend the oak tree 6
    To honor William Stafford 7
    On an Unfamiliar Path 8
    We Come from People 9
    Take off your cloak of mourning; wrap yourself in the stars 10
    Joining the Dance 11
    Tears 12
    Be like a baby 13
    As Darkness Descends 14

II. Graphing Shadow and Light 15
    Suspended Animation 17
    Seeking Solace after Hearing 18
    Like a field 19
    Drawn North 20
    Stonemason's Choices 21
    In the early afternoon 22
    To Recognize Her 23
    Dreams 24
    when faith and hope are sliced away from love 25
    Bless these two 26
    What Remains 27
    Almost Like Time Travel 28

III. Searching for Aquifers 29
    Lullabies after Hiking 31
    November Novena 32
    When the Places We've Been Add Up to More 33
    If you are afraid 34
    Godspeed 35
    For my Younger Son 36
    If Only 38

	Now and Then	40
	She left earth	41
	Cinquain	42
	Approach	43
IV.	Before and Beyond Words	45
	We Are Held by Words	47
	Ebb And Flow	48
	Zounds: abbreviation of God's Wounds	49
	For Children Who Never Talk	50
	You Can't Step Into a Picture	51
	The Words Insist on Taking Their Own Trips	52
	I Can't Describe These Children	53
	Believing Words	54
	To learn a language quickly	55
	Words Once Spoken	56
	The Word	57
V.	Goldfinches Flit. Mockingbirds Sing. Amen	59
	For Whomever	61
	Dancing on My Father's Feet	62
	Two pale pansies	63
	Evading Estrangement	64
	Marsh Mornings	65
	Walk barefoot	66
	Steeplebush	67
	Abide with me	68
	Afraid to Talk to God When Others Are Listening	69
	The purpose of wings	72
	What on Earth	73
	Ghazal Ghazal	74
Acknowledgements		75

I. Beneath Our Common Sky

Queen Anne's Lace   (after William Carlos Williams)

A field of flowers does not need healing
there is the field untrammeled
or there is the field trod over
maybe it is summer

there is the whole summer field
smelling like carrots, buzzing with bees
stiff stems swaying their flat mini-bouquets

there is each flower whole
an aggregate of tiny flowers—
each part its own whole—
and in the surprise center
one purple bloom

there is a person
maybe she has a hand lens
she can touch the rough stem
brush the soft white tops
catch the falling parts
in her other hand

she can bless her hands
give thanks for her hands
feel her hand touching
feel her hand being touched

there is another there
maybe they touch
becoming one yet staying two
there is each person's body
made from many parts
and in each center
a purple beating heart

We Are All in the Waiting Room
(After Elizabeth Bishop)

six years old
walking with Mum
Joanie in a baby carriage
dandelions in the lawn
tulips in Aunt Bridge's garden
all of us breathing in springtime
a blue sky holding us in place
until
big kids ran to my mother   talking all at once
                      a girl just died
     up the street
          12 years old
     an ambulance came   *she had scarlet fever*
               she died
frightened, I looked to my mother
she shushed me
I knew it was something
something bad
something
not to be
mentioned

the air was loud now
planes droning overhead
kids playing in a nearby park
stroller wheels squeaking

it was still springtime
but now I knew
I could die

Anita Coffey Ouellette

I wish I could tell you

I discovered everything—
desert sunrise,
the rocks above tree line,
field grass quaking in the breeze,
the breeze itself, snow.

One morning red-orange light
burned stripes onto an old oak tree.
Cold healed the tree
back into its dismal winter tones

as light changed
into a livable bluish gray
with pale yellow features.

I can't say how to paint radiance.
I know you can breathe it
and walk out into it.

Trees will have their rightful look
separate from the air.
Paths will be lighted.

```
                    All weekend the oak tree
            leans crazily, leans               into the air above my back yard,
    our
            uphill                             neighbor's one-hundred-and-
fifty-foot tree
            at Saturday sunset                         an arborist warns the fall
                                    is imminent
            I read the meaning aloud           *a threat, something hanging over your
head*
            the tree waits for                          air to move or for heat
to swell rot
            lightning                          struck when no one was paying
            attention
we see the split   hear                           cracking, we drag our outside
furniture away
            at night I dream of                forgetting that I owned a horse,  not
feeding it
            of                                 not knowing how to use the brake on an
unfamiliar jeep
            of                        not understanding words cried by a child who didn't
belong to me
            I think                            the tree will
                not                            hit our house
        Monday                              the arborist
        will come                              will cut the tree
        neighbors will watch                will branches
            and  logs               land on
            crush       their own  roots?
        will squirrels and birds
            flee before the fall?
            we will  count the rings,
            firewood will pile up
                free for the taking  today
        we avoid  the back yard, cancel the cookout,
        read Sunday comics away from the windows
```

Anita Coffey Ouellette

To honor William Stafford,

bow to the hawk on the metal roof of a hardware store
hawk's wing-beat, hawk's shadow unseen by
shoppers. Bow to the centenarian
who lives alone, who asks for continued good health
who offers two rum balls, one for the road. Bow
to the branch that flies off, takes the bird feeder with it,
strikes the side of the shed, spills food for squirrels,
for mourning doves. Bow to the aged man
who stands up to greet you. Bow to those who do not
recognize this miracle—one man in hiding
responding to another. Bow to quiet, not a void
to be filled with moving, with talking—listening
no harder than to look beyond the window,
listening no harder than to ride a bicycle across the ice.

Evading Estrangement

On an Unfamiliar Path

I saw a mountain bluebird yesterday
as we approached a mesa just before
a hairpin uphill turn into the sky.

Before an icy wind received my breath
and blew it with approaching storms
I saw a mountain bluebird yesterday

after a dawn as cold as this upland crest
soaring so far above the desert floor
as morning turned uphill into the sky.

If all the blaze-marked trees have disappeared
the trails remain as ravens fly toward home
as mountain bluebirds fly in skies today

unfazed by new clouds bringing unknown weather
above the canyon views as dry winds soar
above the roads that turn into the sky.

Forget-me-nots hold tight to rocky clefts.
Murmuring hot springs solace wintry souls.
I saw a mountain bluebird yesterday
cross clouds and fly beneath our common sky.

Anita Coffey Ouellette

We Come from People

We come from people I search for in graveyards
from the unknown people in my craziest dreams
from people who fought in everyone's civil wars
pacifist people who welcomed strangers home

people who traveled barefoot on stones
who kept the fires at the mouths of caves
who lived in valleys and studied hills

We come from people who couldn't stop singing
people who lived in silence
people who lived in the presence of joy
or of unending sadness

from people who couldn't sit still; who changed their minds
who walked across deserts and over mountains;
people who never left home, never saw oceans
people who traveled across unknown seas

We come from people who built their altars in magical places
who worshipped the sun and listened to gifted prophets
from skeptics, practical builders, quiet people
starving people—people who survived—
from people who remembered all our stories

We come from men and women who passed us our love
for trees, flowers, stones; who feared spiders and snakes
from people who knelt, who prayed by all of our sick beds
people who nurtured frail infants; people who honored the dead
people who lived as long as they could with the living

Evading Estrangement

Take off your cloak of mourning; wrap yourself in the stars

I see the years-ago-us
me behind her
our toy sail boat
becalmed in the mud
each of us
holding a plastic pail
me tall and careful
her tiny and unpredictable
there are no waves
we stand ankle deep
in the low tide at Brewster
where we woke every day
in one August cottage
to the smell of bacon and coffee
to the sound of Dad cooking
still there even at breakfast
our all-day summer vacation
playmate while Mom was mourning—
but we did not know that—
so, there we stand
me behind her
me tall and truthful
except for the day I denied
trying to carry
water in a sieve
to fill the moat of my castle
her tiny and wild
black hair escaping
pony-tails in the wind
wrapped in fog
we're looking out at the ocean
looking for Ireland
which talks to us
in Grandma
and Grandpa's voices
Dad told us later
we wouldn't be able
to see that far—
but we didn't know

Anita Coffey Ouellette

Joining the Dance

I heard a tired mother say to the toddler in the supermarket cart
you can wear your new shoes but you can't dance
my feet wanted to move to that rhythm
I want you to dance for salvation I say
but only in my grandmother mind where all such sayings live
go ahead and dance please dance
dance to the past and future sorrows of all our lives
dance our joys and boredoms
bend wiggle twist move with your thoughts
against your thoughts
dance for the babies you will hold
for the baby you have been
dance for all parents until our words become clear
as we speak our layered shades of meaning
words we don't understand yet speak
dance with nuances in each hand-motion
dance the language of hips
dance at each of your ages
practice dancing as slowly as you will need
to keep your walker steady in the halls of the aged
go to second-hand shops to buy dead peoples' scarves and swirly skirts

rob your mother's closet for gauze or silk
dance for us until we all dance naked or wearing feathers
or wearing antlers found beneath moss
as we join you clothed in our oldest or our best or our only garments
wear your new shoes or no shoes
dance as you did in the womb
as you did as a newborn
as if your classmates will never make you self-conscious
dance as if your mother never said not to

Evading Estrangement

Tears

smiling
I wear crystals
necklaces of salt shards
mined from caves of family history
sparkling

Anita Coffey Ouellette

Be like a baby

whose skin will grow to cover her
    always
        changing
            always the same
                like a lizard
        peeling itself out of each toe
    stepping forth
a brighter color
    for now
        like a river
            dry bedded
                or spilling over its banks
      like anyone
    smiling into the morning rain
or frowning into sunshine.

As Darkness Descends

a peach
ripe on its branch
I choose it
offer it to you

a gust of wind
seen in the grass before it arrives
I stand in it
send it to you

a lilac sprig
many flowers on one bloom
I smell it
hand it to you

an almost empty room
with a blue floral carpet
I unlock the door
furnish it for you

water
to drink and to share
I bless it
pour it for you

children
gathered around a table
I teach them songs
we sing them to you

II. Graphing Shadow and Light

Anita Coffey Ouellette

Suspended Animation

Wait a minute, just you wait, hold your horses, hold your fire. Wait
for the snow to melt, for the leaves to appear in spring, for the drought to end,
for a cease-fire, for a vaccine to arrive, for coups to begin and for coups to end.
All over earth, we wait for first breaths, last breaths, we wait at airports, we
wait for elevators,
for trains, for buses, we wait for the mail to arrive, for phone calls, for election
results. We wait in lines at theaters and at over-crowded clinics. Right now,
somewhere, people wait for water to boil, for the other shoe to drop, for
suspense to end, for a wedding to begin, for a divorce to be
finalized. Starving people are waiting for bread. We wait for children to come
home from
school, for test results, for a race to begin. Anxious people are waiting for job
interviews, waiting for forgiveness, for three-minute eggs to cook,
for a turn at bat, for an ambulance to arrive.
All of us

unbeknownst to each other
all of us together on our common earth
our spinning revolving-waiting-room globe.

Seeking Solace after Hearing

Trying to understand
seated in a shaded garden corner
looking for light

knowing that each day of each season
provides a different amount of sunlight
for each changing square of earth

knowing that sunlight and shadow dance
a daily tango of shifting positions,

I fail again
to graph patterns
of darkness and light.

Anita Coffey Ouellette

Like a field

with hidden quicksand
a glacial erratic
formed under pressure
frozen during an ice age
broken and carried to be here.
I am
like you
like the moon
reflecting different amounts of sunlight
waxing and waning
with a side never seen from earth.

Evading Estrangement

Drawn North

Tiny strawberries
picked and eaten at sunrise
increase our hunger.

Fossilized insects,
lodestones from Arctic islands
balance our canoe.

Wild loud loon cries,
sparks of danger and darkness
hold us together.

Stonemason's Choices

1.
Ice-traveled fire,
cooled into black and silver dots
pink swirling stripes, greens, purples,
compressed sunsets
northern forests,
shapes with no names,
giant's jewels
formed before walls or words,
lost, broken
each boulder
chosen for itself,
a mosaic of prehistory
sandstone and granite
sparkled with feldspar,
mica, quartz.

2.
    A mosaic of ice-traveled fire, shapes with no names
   sandstone, granite, feldspar giant jewels formed before walls
 or words, broken, chipped, perfect, boulders fitted into a pattern
inevitable once formed from the unimagined. Pink, gray, black and white,
stripes, swirls, dots tithed into a collage, pieces of earth's history reorganized.

Evading Estrangement

In the early afternoon

before the thunderstorm
before the sun disappeared
before the hollyhocks blew down
before we shut the windows
we kissed.
Afterwards
we cut down our fallen trees
we studied wildflower books
we dug holes deep enough to hold roots
we surrounded the yucca and prickly pear
with sparkling stones from the beach.

Anita Coffey Ouellette

To Recognize Her

to remedy this   time-crossed
sequencing mishap   I develop backwards
evolving   a negative to my self-portrait
I become her   she becomes me

she gives me time   I focus on her

her face emerges and she sees me in assorted albums

she is listening while I am
singing counterpoint   behind her

Evading Estrangement

Dreams

dress us in each other's faces, put our beds
in other people's rooms. They pull the dead alive.
Dreams lie to us yet teach us what we need to know.

In one dream my words were all in blank verse,
remembered by the note and not the word
if by the note is meant the song
I cannot do without, the reason that the word exists.

Awake, I lost the meaning, searched
for ways to keep the beat
as if motion were life's only need,
its thirst, its driving force,

Maybe dreaming wisdom says to rest
inhabit space, and search from inside
those clouds surrounding us trusting
that truth will always find its songs.

when faith and hope are sliced away from love

there are mornings full of
purple nightshade flowers
with their yellow beak-shaped centers
when the webs of orb-weave spiders
hold their shiny drops of dew
before the unsuspecting butterflies
are trapped

the day before the hurricane
we built the beach's finest castle
we decorated turrets
with small pieces of rose quartz
and we plastered all the walls
with perfect broken shells

Bless these two,

brothers, so
different, so
the same.
Torn from
the same
page of history,
bodies remembering
the same
grandmothers
the same
grandfathers, so
loved by
the same
God, by
the same
parents,
so bathed in
the same
light,
so covered by
different
shadows,
so different
from each other,
so the same.

Anita Coffey Ouellette

What Remains

We have walked hand in hand
as leaves lost their green
as frost whitened our summer chairs

We know that tree roots can break through concrete.

As faraway islands drown in the deepening sea
as trees fall in forests unnoticed by either of us
we shelter warm and safe at our fireside.

We have listened to the silence left after every snowfall.

As weakness becomes as likely as strength
as stars can't be seen in the ever-bright night
we remember the smiles of our long-ago babies

their cries and the ways that we comforted them.

Almost Like Time Travel

1.
New roots, grow, grasp,
attach
wherever they are

2.
He loved to laugh
even at his own jokes.
His easy laughter left
when he lost his words.
His life rearranged itself
as smiling emerged
for other peoples' jokes.

3.
here, now, this
not
there, then, that

4.
Sunlight streams in windows
at the wrong times of day
here, on a dead-end road
bordered by dense woods
where only winter branches
open the sky,
no longer there, on a hilltop
with an unobstructed view.

5.
not where we were
we find ourselves
together, still
where we are

III. Searching for Aquifers

Anita Coffey Ouellette

Lullabies after Hiking

On a mountain trail
sleeping in a three-sided Adirondack shelter
there were human sounds

hikers zipping, unzipping sleeping bags
fabric covers rustling,
sleepers tossing and turning,

and quiet conversations not quite heard
intonation carrying the weight
ordinarily borne by words.

this murmuring of strangers
like lullabies in someone else's language,
all need for understanding vanished

November Novena

When sunset looks like embers
lambent light against encroaching darkness
a silent novena might be begun for enemies

a quick prayer a day for the next nine days
prayers that our enemies be seen
as they were when new-born
helpless, appealing, needy, cared-for

a daily prayer that each one be loved
as on those earlier days
when crying still meant
mother's milk would be coming
and blankets would swaddle.

Anita Coffey Ouellette

When the Places We've Been Add Up to More

When storms appear and caves become the driest place
and sitting in an ancient beehive hut brings ease

when canyon walls cast shadows on the river rocks
and cupping hands beneath a waterfall releases thirst

when ghosts reveal themselves in broken earthenware
and bending backward shows you cobalt skies and cactus thorns

when flowers group themselves in natural bouquets
and forlorn-feeling places reappear in sunlight

when meadowlarks come back to nest on Midwest prairies
and spiders are as yellow as the buttercups they walk on

when remembered cellos and pianos have arrived
and music brings you right to meadows, moors, and mesas

when inchworms match the blades of grass they sway with
and deer are safely hidden just beyond the tree line

then we need nothing else, as you and I stay blessed
by breathing color-saturated air with all.

Evading Estrangement

If you are afraid

of the eye of the world
do you also

close one eye
or squint through both,

hold your hand
against the sky

or look down? If you
hold a scarf

over your face
and look up

even through silk
aren't the trees leaning

toward light
and aren't all creatures

even when blinded
and burrowing

isn't every
living thing

seeking light
or running away?

Anita Coffey Ouellette

Godspeed

This town keeps its children
from Northern seas.
This town tells you.
Lie down in Bermuda.
Take off your hat.
Cut your hair.

You love the Arctic.
I love your peaks and valleys.
Here we live in a temperate zone.
Go North. Fare well. Be careful.
The elements where you will travel are fierce.
You need the protection your hair and your hat give.

You are like an iceberg—
what's underneath causes danger at night
and in solar eclipses.
Jagged with powerful peaks
filled with fresh water,
icebergs save thirsty sailors
waiting for currents to free them.

Evading Estrangement

For my Younger Son

In late afternoon
green spruce needles change
into sharp black shadows,
startling for a few moments,
against purple-bordered orange.
   The glow of imagined light,
     heat from remembered light,
     peace from old light,
   help me see.
My feet tread
at the steady treadmill pace.
The cold, the dark,
the bare branches are gone.
I see light fused.

December floodlights merge
with the light of June sunsets.
Four o'clock is the same
as eight o'clock.
You and I are ageless.
   The glow of imagined light,
     heat from remembered light,
     peace from old light,
   help me see.
I tread at this steady pace.
You tend to other children
learning most children live,
some children die, all children
disappear to be rediscovered.

A violet's stem casts a shadow
on late August afternoons.
Trunks of old-growth trees hide
inside moonless Advent nights.

My feet tread
at this steady pace.
I see journey-pieces unreeling,
spliced into family stories.

Anita Coffey Ouellette

The glow of imagined light,
heat from remembered light,
peace from old light,
help me see.

Once, on a forest trail at dusk
you mimed imagined injury—
uncontrollable writhings,
incoherent mumblings—
I screamed at you to stop it.

On another day at dawn
in a clearing by the stream
a deer leapt between us
and stopped there
for a long moment,
startling me forever.

If Only:

I could find the cemeteries where parts of me are buried, the ones with crumbling stones with missing and broken headstones or with no headstones, where I would say *Thank you, I'm sorry,   I wish I knew you all at least by your names*, and in one of these graveyards I would find a shining obelisk with my great-grandmother's name engraved on it, I would be there on her birthday, purely by chance, with my cousin beside me

I could live near the caldera, the one that I never hiked into, in that Jemez Mountain town where the bar looked like part of a Western movie and I saw someone thrown out onto the street and it wasn't even on poker night and you walked every day to the coffee shop while I wrote my best Villanelle in the house with glass walls where we saw mountain bluebirds and we didn't worry about rattlesnakes

We could hike like we used to, baby in backpack, four year old happy beside us except when he was so scared, shrieking on a high-grassed mountain ridge where it looked like we could fall into the vastness and it was too steep to carry him so I sat, scooted down over the grass with him behind me his arms tight around me, his eyes closed against my back until we reached the safety of aspen trees and I knew I could protect him, but this was before he grew up to be a mountain climber

I could go to Baffin Island live for the summer in a tent, the constant sunshine on snow would not give me migraines, you would be with me, Mike would be our guide, you would have a rifle which you would use to keep polar bears away and I would find arctic flowers in melting crevices for Amy to photograph, she and I would arrange photos and poems together in the book we will publish and you and I would sleep in our zipped-together sleeping bags where we are never cold

You and I could go to Greenland for one year, live in a red house with Pete and CC and Josh and we would learn from our neighbors how to live in ice and snow, in the extremes of day and night, we would deal with mud, with fewer fruits and vegetables, we would use more candles and none of us would be bored, all of us would keep journals, refuse to know what was happening outside of our rented neighborhood, before we returned to our separate lives

I could visit every place I've ever lived, be with the people who lived there with me and in one place I would sit on the ground beneath the old lilac tree, its low-hanging branches hiding me in that house where I was always alone

And in another place, I would wander into that meadow where the moss underfoot was always wet in the morning, where I would stand in a golden field sometimes with Joan, our baby brother asleep inside with Mum, and I, lulled for while by buzzing and humming, found the tall pink flowers that I studied for years before I wrote the poem called Steeplebush, long, long before any of us died..

Evading Estrangement

Now and Then

Now is enough
beech trees outside my windows
ancient moss-covered stumps
in the forest clearings
a vernal pond
where wood frogs sing
on late winter days

but I am greedy

for a summer field
with bees buzzing purple clover
yellow spiders on buttercups
midst the sound
of mountain winds, greedy
for the children who played
there with blowing hair
in the undulating grass.

Anita Coffey Ouellette

She left earth

as lightning
blazing against
the rippled pond
illuming
a hilltop into
zig-zagged
halves.

Dancing a path
through
a thunder cloud
she escaped
the limits of air.

Evading Estrangement

Cinquain

Him, me
shadowed by ghosts
pieces of our shared past
strings of glass beads strung between us
blurring

Approach

We walked on muddy trails during mountain cloudbursts
to get to this sunshine.
Directly beneath us, roots branch over granite
                            searching for aquifers.
Wind bends leaf-laden boughs into cumulous skies.
                            I wait at the tree line
hugging a slanting trunk as paper birch bark slaps
                            against my cold fingers.
Mapping a future rock climb, my husband and son
agree on safe handholds.
                            The wind takes their voices.
The sharp lichened cliff face rises above the trees
a wall for grabbing against with fingers and toes.
                            I watch emptiness change.
Tied together they are drinking the same blue air.

IV. Before and Beyond Words

Anita Coffey Ouellette

We Are Held by Words

carved into mountain rocks
beech trees and wedding rings

exchanged as hands are shaken
as the air is stilled or moved

dependent upon a listener
subject to misinterpretation

tethered by their presence
and by their absence

Ebb And Flow

Nushu
a women's language
died
its oldest writer Yang Huanyi
gone in 2004
sad to say
no readers left

take heart
other women's languages
reborn each day
will always be written between spoken lines
where brides are feted or consoled
babies blessed or buried

women's words kept alive
by a river of eye blinks and smiles
by tapestries of curlicues and squiggles
by what mothers teach

in Kenya in Central China
in Afghanistan in Florida
women are reading and writing
in the vernacular of life

it's time to
sprinkle the secret dictionaries
with shredded lies
cover the casketed poems
with petals and snowflakes
let Wangare Maathai sprinkle the ashes
over the whirling earth

Yang Huanyi is dead
Long live Wangare Maathai

Anita Coffey Ouellette

Zounds: abbreviation of God's Wounds

Babies who will speak
all sound alike
babies who will speak Amharic
and babies who will speak French
babble each other's phonemes,

sounds their parents smile at,
sound boundaries
between baby and parent
greater than those between baby and baby.

For babies who will speak
refining the boundaries between
speech sounds

proceeds as if destined.
Babies who will speak
leap from ba to da to

abracadabra with glottal clicks
bound for whatever home
they inhabit
and children who don't talk
don't say "Mom" or "Dad" don't say "more"
or "help" or "no"
Unthinkable.

Impossible.
This wound
cannot be
abbreviated.

For Children Who Never Talk

When the pathways
through a tangled wilderness
have never been made
there is no place to walk
so you clear away brambles
even though you get scratched
place stones across streams
even though the way remains slippery

When being silent is not their choice
connections form
before and beyond words

Anita Coffey Ouellette

You Can't Step Into a Picture

I hold his hand, his shadow runs
over unfamiliar sites. He's blind
to shadows and to certain structures
although he reads fine print and he sees

the invisible. I always notice his blindness
but never mention or understand it
because he reads fine print and sees
those people who enter his space to greet him.

I never mention my misunderstanding.
I don't get the chance because he confuses
people who enter his space with gremlins,
with cough drops and CAT scan machines.

I watch him amusing, amazing, scaring
those people who enter his space. With greetings
and more cough drops I soothe him for now.
He never mentions our misunderstandings.

The Words Insist on Taking Their Own Trips

A child I talk with answers with a hiss
I translate into words: "Watch out. Beware.
Don't listen. Read my face." I do not miss
the look of apprehension often there.
The language of his eyes can be so spare
I read his fear, confusion, overload.
Not understanding makes him prone to stare
at fences, twirling fingers, lines in roads.
His brain is made from tangled strands. Words slowed
in passing through the air digress, detour
to places that they've been before. They goad
his memory causing speech to flow. Unsure
of what he means—*him*/*me* connections missed
again—I show him books. We will persist.

Anita Coffey Ouellette

I Can't Describe These Children

1.
an anemone
born in a midnight sea
stretching toward the amazing sun
gently waving in darkness
unobserved

                        2.
              neon explosions
       bright breath-taking patterns
      formed in a wilderness sky
     fireworks spelling out answers
              unwitnessed

                                              3.
                            a turquoise iceberg
                         filled with aqua flowers
                       floating near the equator
             cooling angelfish as they swim
                                unaware

Believing Words

I saw what I was told was the sky
and so I thought it was real
always
a hard, blue cover over us wherever we were
a darkened night-time boundary
holding in sun, moon, stars

I saw that sometimes
clouds blocked our view
but I thought
the sky stayed there above the clouds
just waiting for storms to end

at seven
other disillusionments were coming
adults can be wrong
earthquakes and volcanoes are real
dragons are not
children can die

but nothing surprised me,
as much as being told
in a most matter-of-fact correction
that, oh no, there is no actual sky
no ceiling covering us
holding everything in, no,
just space which is sort of like air
that never ends
an emptiness that isn't even blue

Anita Coffey Ouellette

To learn a language quickly

you go to that country
where you don't know
where they don't understand
where greeting strangers is required/forbidden

they look at you as if you were wrong
when only yesterday you thought you were right
the trip back home has been canceled
because
it's just your job to stay here now

live where people drive
on the other side of the street
where animals don't respond to their names
where you can't yell for help
except by falling and lying in silence

you accept that country
you live there quietly
gaze lowered ears alert
you learn to speak
your new language
even though you dream
in the language you learned
in your mother's house

Words Once Spoken

Wicked
anger. Damned voice
pretending to be me,
yelling, scattering poisoned words
holding

throbbing
anger, pumping
words to starve love with. Stop.
Sprinkle sorrow into midnight.
Stroll wrapped,

chastened,
in penitence.
Whisper memories. Hear.
Draw the lines you won't step over.
Again.

Anita Coffey Ouellette

The Word

I want to apologize once and for all.
I'm sorry for saying sorry too often—
sorry for *excuse me*, for *I don't understand*,
sorry when you bump me or I bump you.
I'm sorry for silence, for thinking
that wars always happen,
that time can be wasted.

I need to say *sorry* for once and for all,
to the sky and marsh for not keeping
their greens and blues inside me,
to the hawk for seeing
its hiding place in the pine,
to snow for not hearing it fall,
to you for my believing that
anyone owns the shoreline.

I'm sorry for not saying sorry enough.
I need to find a child in Mexico,
a little girl coughing and holding
her hand out, to whom I say,
Donde esta su casa? Lo siento.
I need to talk to the dead, to the ones
I lived with, to say *I'm sorry.*
I didn't believe you were old.

I need to go to a church I prayed in,
a church where I'll pray again,
to stop kneeling, to stand in protest
when the deacon preaches nonsense,
when he thinks he understands God.
Sorry has a rhythm and a meaning
I need to feel in my feet to dance
down an aisle with. *Sorry, sorry, sorry.*
for once and for all.

V. Goldfinches Flit. Mockingbirds Sing.
Amen

For Whomever

of my friends remembered
named for me the flowers in books, vases, gardens
goldfinches flit, mockingbirds sing.   I bend

my head, then send the seen and overheard—
ferns, toads, spider's webs, thunder's laments—
to whomever of my remembered friends
I feel nearby in woods, meadows, gardens

Still teaching the nameless me, attaching words
to cactus, honeysuckle, oxygen,
lightning, poison ivy, milkweed, cairns, wind.
For whomever of my friends remembered,
named the flowers in wild and tame gardens
goldfinches flit, mockingbirds sing. Amen.

Evading Estrangement

Dancing on My Father's Feet

This is and isn't a fairy tale
about a knight named Walter
and an unnamed tyrant,
a knight born with fairy-tale armor,
born with a gift unmatched in the kingdom,
born with what he himself described after he died
as extreme kindness.

Most people would say kindness in the extreme,
placing-a-blown-off- peony-on-a-lily-pad kindness,
comical-eulogy-kindness.
The unnamed tyrant ordered Walter to give up his gift
of drying-your-wet-shoes-and-socks-kindness,
planting-yellow-flag-Iris-beside-the-water-garden kindness,
but the tea-and-soda-bread-with-butter-kindness,
joking-while-being-bandaged kindness continued,
the knight's only act of disobedience.

The tyrant banished the knight,
sent magicians to torture Walter
who forgave the tyrant,
treated the magicians with putting-you-in-the-parade kindness,
not-seeing-embarrassing tears kindness,
every-last-bit-of-the-gift-he-was-born-with kindness
until once upon a time he died.

Anita Coffey Ouellette

Two pale pansies

blue-streaked held in
a wineglass filled with
water on the white
window shelf alone
on the shelf in front
of the screen
in the kitchen greenhouse window, the screen the window the pansies
see? Wind from the north at night after the heat wave after her death
after the storm that tore down David's totem pole the wind through the
screen over the top of the wineglass the wind the glass the pansies, see?
Two pale blue-streaked pansies blown from the wineglass onto the new
windowsill painted white after the heat wave two years after the storm
after her death
blown there
lying there lying
there in the morning
in the kitchen on
the wide window shelf
in front of the wine
glass now filled only
with water, petals pale
and blue-streaked, thin
green stems two flowers
lying there out of water
lying across each other
the totem pole and
the sign of the cross, see?

Evading Estrangement

In my church stained-glass glows
light streams through red, blue and purple,
yearnings bordered in black
at my friend's funeral, her rabbi speaks of Sabbath,
says the most common phrase in the Bible is

    Do not be afraid

shells exploded in a mosque
leaving ruined walls, unintended shapes
for the never-inured-from-shock,
spider webs and daisies now flourish
beneath absent roofs

    Kneel

on every beach, seaweed hooks
to iridescence, tangled shells chime
beneath wave-driven water. Granite carried
from the beach seems to disappear
when sedums cover it with green

    Look up

clouds
flow across the tops of masts
drift above this earth, seen even from
space, leaving interrupted
glimpses of blue

Marsh Mornings

when mud changes place twice daily with water
when salt water nourishes tough marsh grass
when grass hides foxes and hungry herons
when heron wings beat and hummingbirds hover
when hummingbirds land in the dying geranium plant
when wild plants end at sand then sea then horizon
when the horizon is seen through changing colors
when colors include the color of rain
when rain arrives without or with wind
when wind arranges morning fog
when morning fog almost burns off
when burning off has a gentle meaning
when meaning hums like a faraway foghorn
when foghorns bleat across acres of mud

Evading Estrangement

Walk barefoot

Every day.
Walk on carpets
on wood floors
stone, tile
branch out
onto grass, moss, dirt
stand for a minute on snow and ice
take a few steps on gravel
keep moleskin in your pocket
for ragged skin or blisters
return to easier ground
but stay
rooted.

Rub your feet on any smooth surface
notice the charge that builds up.

We are like rain clouds
just before lightning
seeking balance
from the earth.

Anita Coffey Ouellette

Steeplebush

Bowled-over by a flower—a plume of pink almost as tall as
I was, a seven-year-old new to the countryside, surprised

by discovering these soft spikes filled with countless miniature
flowers, finding out slowly that they would bloom all summer long

Drawn to this meadow next to my house, drawn outside
where the ground was uneven, mossy and often wet

where I was alone to observe this countless
bounty, so many flowers within each spire

where each separate blossom glowed when the sun was right,
where tiny insects crawled, where I was

surrounded by clouds of pink, by buzzing bees
in an early morning meadow island of joy

Abide with me,

said the hummingbird to me
but I, said I, *can't fly you see. And you
don't talk.* So back to where I started from,
frightened here, before the stream whose shallow
stepping stones have disappeared beneath
the surge from last night's storm. *Where did you go
when lightning came with roaring wind?* Stopping
here as I have beside you as you drink from
nearby hyssop blossoms, still I wonder

will I cross this stream, not knowing yet
the depth, assuming shallow, yes, of course
but still my boots, my socks, my feet will not
stay dry. Accustomed as I am to comfort
this presents a daunting choice: to stay
here, still, to think about your flight, about

the magic of your hovering, your wings
that tip in alternating dips, about
the vortices that this creates the whirls
the swirls confessing here that vortices
remain mysterious to me, imagined like
the eddies in a rushing stream, the ones
that grab and tip canoes and dump the gear—
or *will I be moved by your existence,
will I stand, walk through moving water?*

Anita Coffey Ouellette

Afraid to Talk to God When Others Are Listening

I.
Osprey,
we hold our babies
as you nurture chicks who cry in your nest.

Fierce-fisher,
you plunge feet first, pluck a fish from
its school, drop it before
you get to your young. Gulls scavenge, push their beaks into
your lost prize.

Nest-maker,
you build your debris-and-stick home above
muck on a man-made stanchion. Each year you
fly to this finite marsh framed by boaters,
beach-goers, walkers, bird watchers raising
binoculars, you in the crosshatches.

Wild-bird,
one of your offspring lies dead, head missing,
torn by dogs after its fall. Didn't you
teach it to fly? When hurricanes come,
will you be away?

Hoverer,
I cup water, stay still, eyes and toes to
clouds. Separated by the air we breathe,
belly toward belly, wrist, and elbow-arms
toward wrist and elbow-wings, beak toward nose, we
mirror each other. Suspended over
the same sea bottom, I face empty sky,
you see sky reflected in bright ocean.

Friend,
if you were gone, schools of minnows would jump
to silver a moment of air, clouds would
shadow shallows; we
would watch the heron and egret. The dark hole
of your absence would be another

unnamed frontier. You, your mottled bent wings,
your talons, your black-marked wrists,
would be forgotten.

II.
Human,
I see you. I see you
standing there. I
fly over you. You
pray to the wrong god,
my wings, my shadow,
the talons you praise
are made as your arms,
and your grasping hand.

I see you. I hear
your toes grabbing sand
when a small wave rocks you,
I feel the pulse
as you float on waves,
I smell you, I taste
your sweat in my food.
I am no stanchion
for you to build on.

I speak by living.
Can you hear the thump
of my wings, the small cries
of my hatchlings,
the apology
my talons speak while
they strike the sea bass?
Do you smell blood
in the water, taste
salt in the wind, as I
swoosh over your
upturned face? You will
hear the vacuum left
when I don't return.
Be content when
my shadow startles you.

III.
What are the questions a child can think of?
Why have I forgotten them?

IV.
Parent
praise the child who watches. She is you.

Fragile companion,
the ground is spongy. See red leaves on
poison ivy; blueberries next to
goldenrod, sea lavender, rose hips,
second petals all dusted with ice.

Naked observer,
 wear green against autumn, blue against
sunshine, yellow and white against rain,
against night. Be released from comfort
into oak tree, asters, seaweed, salt,
wood smoke, water, mud, sweat, be as snow
in summer wind, as lightning in fog.

Wanderer,
quiet after watching yellow and
pink meadow flowers; sit on your rock,
look beside you at the bushes where
clusters formed from the smallest flowers
will dry in place until spring comes back.

The purpose of wings:
                          to rest
                pleated shut against small bodies
                      folded feathers
    to keep the heart beating

  in storms, in darkness
to stretch over eggs or hatchlings or wounded mates
                to unfold at dawn in surprising swirls
  to fluff in the presence of enemies
to flock rising on updrafts

one bird looking like all the others
              veering   spiraling
              angling
      wing-marking maps above the horizon
              many as one,
as one giant bird seeks south.

Anita Coffey Ouellette

What on Earth

I fear I am about to die as I
may be, as you may be. We understand.

We are not humpback whales stranded
on a Cape Cod shore; we have foresight

reprieve, before the worldwide suicide
we could foretell. Even time we squander

gives us space to live, to give, to spend,
to lose, to save. Each day will see a noontide

that can be recognized. Those whales
in arctic currents, luminous beluga,

swimming in a changing sea, grow
old in time that kills, that heals. Their ways

depend on how we hope. We can make hoops
for Noah's creatures all to pass through. So...

Evading Estrangement

Ghazal Ghazal

Any answer has its *on the other hand*.
I accept this truth except about your hands.

Communion is given by a minister's hands.
The first eucharist came from a savior's hands.

The house they love is in another's hands.
The strength to wrest it free is in their hands.

A well-run ship feeds oranges to her hands.
A hurricane requires every sailor's hands.

Hanging on the wall, there, prints of their hands—
their names—Peter and Michael, brother's hands.

What we are told not to have: borrower's hands.
What we are told not to have: lender's hands.

Remember watching him shave with father's hands?
Remember watching her weave with mother's hands?

Blessings come from the beauty of his hands, her hands.
Fall asleep holding each other's beautiful hands.

I need a bottled message styled by your hands.
I swear to this and sign in my own hand.

Acknowledgements

<u>Avocet</u>: Online *Marsh Mornings*
<u>Bear Creek Haiku:</u> *Cinquain (Him, Me)*
<u>Bellowing Ark:</u> *For my Younger Son, November Novena, Now and Then, Queen Anne's Lace*
<u>Burning Bright</u> (anthology): *The Word*
<u>Hawk and Whippoorwill:</u> *On an Unfamiliar Path*
<u>Orbis:</u> *Approach, Ebb and Flow, If You are afraid, When the Places We've Been Add Up to More, We Come from People* (previously titled *All of Us*)
Over the Edge Poetry Contest (runner-up): *Afraid to Talk to God*
<u>Passager:</u> *The Purpose of Wings, The Word*
<u>The Curlew:</u> *Abide with Me*
<u>The Lyric:</u> *For Whomever*
<u>My Heart Your Soul…A Collection of Poems Inspired by Autism</u>: *I Can't Describe These Children to People Who Do Not Know Them* was published in an anthology compiled by Nannette Ohman, copyright 1995, Autism Society of America
<u>the new renaissance:</u> *When faith and Hope Are Sliced Away from Love*
<u>The Penwood Review:</u> *Godspeed*
<u>Unlocking the Poem</u> (Anthology): *All weekend the oak tree*
<u>Worcester Review</u> (First Prize Annual Poetry Contest): *Ghazal Ghazal*

www.ingramcontent.com/pod-product-compliance
Lightning Source LLC
LaVergne TN
LVHW090039090426
835510LV00038B/899